This collection is dedicated to the hope that someday, somehow, this span of man's time on earth will all make sense.

WAR

Alessandro Manzetti
Marge Simon

Illustrated by Stefano Cardoselli

Let the world know:
#IGotMyCLPBook!

Crystal Lake Publishing
www.CrystalLakePub.com

Copyright 2018 Crystal Lake Publishing

All Rights Reserved

Property of Crystal Lake Publishing

ISBN: 978-1-64316-771-8

Cover Art:
Wendy Saber Core

Layout:
Lori Michelle—www.theauthorsalley.com

This is a work of fiction. Names, characters, businesses, places, events and incidents are either the products of the authors' imaginations or used in a fictitious manner. Any resemblance to actual persons, living or dead, or actual events is purely coincidental.

No part of this publication may be reproduced, stored in a retrieval system, or transmitted in any form or by any means, without the prior permission in writing of the publisher, nor be otherwise circulated in any form of binding or cover than that in which it is published and without a similar condition including this condition being imposed on the subsequent purchaser.

"Night of Tears" was originally published in *HWA Poetry Showcase Vol. 3*

"George Tecumseh Sherman's Ghost" was originally published in *Silver Blade 32*.

Welcome to another Crystal Lake Publishing creation.

Thank you for supporting independent publishing and small presses. You rock, and hopefully you'll quickly realize why we've become one of the world's leading publishers of Dark and Speculative Fiction. We have some of the world's best fans for a reason, and hopefully we'll be able to add you to that list really soon. Be sure to sign up for our newsletter to receive two free eBooks, as well as info on new releases, special offers, and so much more. To follow us behind the scenes while supporting independent publishing and our authors, be sure to follow us on Patreon.

Welcome to Crystal Lake Publishing—Tales from the Darkest Depths.

Other poetry collections by Alessandro Manzetti:

VENUS INTERVENTION (with Corrine De Winter)
EDEN UNDERGROUND
SACRIFICIAL NIGHTS (with Bruce Boston)
NO MERCY

Other poetry collections by Marge Simon:

NIGHT SMOKE (with Bruce Boston)
VECTORS: A WEEK IN THE DEATH OF A PLANET (with C. Jacob)
VAMPIRES, ZOMBIES, AND WANTON SOULS
DANGEROUS DREAMS
SWEET POISON (with Mary Turzillo)
FOUR ELEMENTS (with L. Addison, C. Jacob and R. Graves)
SMALL SPIRITS: DARK DOLLS
NAUGHTY LADIES
SATAN'S SWEETHEARTS (with Mary Turzillo)

CONTENTS

1	THE GREEN LADY
3	LADY D'ARBANVILLE
6	THE FIRST MANDINGO WAR: 1883
9	SUMMERTIME
10	VUKOVAR'S GHOSTS
14	SPLEEPING MOLOCH
16	SPECTRAL PERFUME
17	HUSH
20	NIGHT OF TEARS
22	IRAQI SUNSET
23	GEORGE TECUMSEH SHERMAN'S GHOST
26	THE BLACK SENTRY
28	ALICE IN HELL
33	WHITE SIEGE
36	THE SOUTHERN LADY
37	MISS SAIGON
40	TEN TO ONE
42	THE GHOSTS OF CULLODEN: 1746
44	THE MAN WHO WOULD BE KING
47	THE LONG WALK TO HELL
49	ONE NIGHT STAND
51	THE CEMETERY WAR: BOOT HILL
53	POP 9/11
56	DRUG WARS: FOUR POEMS

61	BLACK RAY
63	CHOCOLATES FOR TWINS
66	HOLY DIVER
69	THE CASTRATO'S PARADE
71	YBYI 21

Alessandro Manzetti
Marge Simon

WAR

War, n. A by-product of peace

—Ambrose Bierce

THE GREEN LADY
by Alessandro Manzetti and Marge Simon

In this forever jungle; death hangs
almost palpable in the humidity.
Never mind the napalm—
if you don't get bitten by snakes,
it'll be one of their goddam insects you can't see,
like the one that got the kid from Kansas,
bloodsucker's poison went straight to his heart.

We've got smokes, we've got weed
and some other stuff, but no acid, man,
this surreal hell is on the US army.

Twilight's the worst—there comes
a silence terrible and incomplete,
when your piss freezes
in nighty-five degrees.

Snipers in the bushes,
you can't see them, but you know
someone's going to take a hit—
you pray it won't be you.

Finally morning comes,
time to move out, Sarge's order,
so we do, each on our own weird trip, man—
a Ulysses patrol and one Siren,
I guess make that *my* Siren.
Now I see you, now I don't
but I know you're following me,
I hear your feet stepping on branches,
the click of your pointy rice-grain teeth,

your voice inside my helmet,
a Harpy's song, like the sea in a shell.

Through a glimpse of multi-foliage I see
your smooth green thighs opening slowly,
a purple vanda orchid blooming, shaking its petals,
its stamen beckoning like a lover's tongue,
but you disappear again.

Now I see you, now I don't,
but I know you're making yourself beautiful,
combing your vine green hair,
while we sink to the waist,
wade these black waters
holding our rifles over our heads
as if surrending to your beauty—
but wait, this is my fantasy alone,
each of us must have his own.

Now I see you, now I don't.
Nightfall, we're still on the move,
and as some beguiled and crazy Wise Man,
I see between the heads of the trees
your dazzling napalm star.

Maybe you're back in your Mekong
fishing for dead bodies floating,
going through their pockets,
scattering black-and-white photos to the wind,
kissing Viet Kong soldiers one by one

as they glide through the mangroves.
Many linger in your sultry uterus
absorbed into your verdant hell,
while the helicopters of the living
slice the clouds, searching casualites,
all for nothing.

LADY D'ARBANVILLE
by Alessandro Manzetti and Marge Simon

Paris June 14, 1940

She enters his room,
slender legs encased in silky net,
small flowers caught in webbed designs,
stockings most women would sell their bodies for,
but she is not most women.

A single diamond on a chain around her throat,
faux gems woven in her hair, a shade of blonde
that has to be real as her gray eyes,
the color of ash on war torn ruins.

My Lady D'Arbanville, why do you sleep so still?
I'll wake you when the tanks move further on,
when the blasts and the bleat of shots dies down
and the moon is low in the western sky.

You think you've taken Paris,
but I assure you we're not done.
Das Fuhrer is a monster, soldier boy.

My Lady D'Arbanville, I know it's you,
my comrades brag they've had you many times,
but with you in my arms, their words I can't believe.
They say French girls are easy, pay them in cigarettes.

But all you ask is to kiss my Iron Cross—
liebchen, das Eisernes Kreuz is yours,
for just this night, I place it in your hand.
and drink your wine until my mind is fogged,
tell you anything you ask.

ALESSANDRO MANZETTI AND MARGE SIMON

The dawn is near and you must go,
but first let's lift another glass,
and I will spread my legs once more.

My Lady D'Arbanville, sleeping on so still?
Why do you pretend to lie as dead?
Wake and move beneath my loins again,
kiss my chest and grasp my neck,
for dawn is coming soon and I must go.

My brother is résistant Joseph Barthele,
he rages that your men have such contempt,
a scorn that sears us deeply, soldier boy.

My Lady D'Arbanville, open your eyes!
I pull up my pants, put on my boots,
and take the hand of my friend winter,
who follows me everywhere,
blowing horrendous thoughts into my ears.

We've cut the Eiffel Tower's cables,
your swastika will never fly so high,
nor any flag besides our own, soldier boy.

My Lady D'Arbanville, still you slumber!
I must resume patrol on your black-and-white city,
while from your brothels' balconies, laughter—
champagne pours down into the streets
cleansing the night of what we've done.

It is you who sleeps now, soldier boy.
Cold and clean as winter wind, this dagger's kiss,
et merci for your secrets, solider boy.

She leaves his room,
slender legs encased in silky net,
small flowers caught in webbed designs,

WAR

confounding eyes that linger there,
the Lady D'Arbanville.

THE FIRST MANDINGO WAR: 1883
by Marge Simon

I am Samory Tour of the Niger-Congo,
head of all Mandingo warriors.
My fingers are long,
my ears hear all over the world,
and my vision spans centuries.

The English call the Frenchmen frogs,
a term for their disgusting culinary tastes.
We call them other things,
knowing little of their history and caring less,
just as they have treated us.

We ride the Arab ponies, bred by our own,
attuned to touch of heel or hand and fleet of foot.
They dance away from sabers, bullets, threats.

Louis-Gustave arrives in Kong astride an ox,
his men follow with a line of burdened asses.
I'm told an attendant trims his tiny mustache,
applies ointment to his pale cheeks
to hinder the mosquitoes.

The frogs hide in the bushes
I hear the croak and lock of rifles.
In the early morning steam off the Niger,
sun at our backs, we move forward.

By dusk, the river's shores are stained
garnet leaked from their black uniforms.
This "Cote d' Ivories" was never theirs to name.

WAR

Our ruined villages, my testament to war.
My men leave nothing of use behind.
No crops, no animals, no regrets.
Better to destroy our world
than give it to the frogs.

SUMMERTIME
by Alessandro Manzetti

inspired by Wolfe's Look Homeward, Angel

Somewhere in August 1915.

O lost, and by the wind grieved ghost,
come back again, get close
to the rest of your bombed family.
And you, Angel, look the other way
and hold your nose.
Summer, with its hungry flies
is entering the trenches,
dreadful as its blurred horizons,
continually shifting to expose
the front line of Hell
ignited by a black sun.
O lost, and by bullets riddled ghost,
collect the hundreds of eyes
of your new brothers,
roll them around like marbles;
put them together, make a necklace
and wear it now.
You're so beautiful.
You will see in the distance
hundreds of empty houses,
hidden doors, and all the faces
they have loved and lost.

VUKOVAR'S GHOSTS
by Alessandro Manzetti and Marge Simon

November 20, 1991

If you're looking for ghosts,
just raise your eyes
towards the rusty top
of this water tower;
we're all there, sitting
around invisible tables
of an abandoned restaurant
floating above the city
and the red dust
which shows, intermittently,
the bunch of Arkan's tigers
with their all black stripes.

First, they came for our women—
we even knew some of them,
and screamed out their names
to tone deaf ears and feral eyes.

They took our daughters,
then mothers the same, making all watch,
over and over until they were tired,
blood from between so many legs
staining the pavements
in an unholy menstruation.

Among the living is a woman
who testifies how she asked her husband to leave,
but he would not go, though he knew
what had been done to her,
scarring her soul as it had her body,

WAR

emptying her of passion,
useless as our water tower.

In front of our mouths
there is a dish of grenades
with a side of back bacon,
gunpowder and fresh memories
just juiced from hundred of heads.
—so clear and exquisite—
You can join us,
we're drinking bourbon
distilled from boiled blood
and we're still waiting for the dessert,
tha armistice, the silence
and a fat sunset.

We are all twins, born at the same time
in the Ovčara farm
six miles away from here,
into shouting's storage hangars,
thanks to a bullet in the head
rabid, rapid, cold as the mud
which is watertight in the ditches,
all round, where the frogs sing
the Death March,
giving the illusion of being in a dream,
perhaps in a forest in Madagascar,
—all those camouflage suits—
—and the choir of the amphibians—
and still be alive, definitely,
with a loaf of bread between the teeth
instead of a tongue frozen by fear.

Join us as we toast
the living and the dead
with our special bourbon,

floating high above the city
and the red, red dust.

SLEEPING MOLOCH
by Alessandro Manzetti

September 1914

Moloch! Solitude! Filth! Ugliness!
'What the fuck . . . ' the beast growls.
Moloch whose mind is pure machinery!
Moloch whose blood is running money!
The blue mosquitoes of the future
are sucking the monster's blood,
shooting in its brain (as big as a sperm whale)
through electric arrows of images,
a phantom voice and the silhouette
—fat and naked and so funny—
of a long-bearded miniaturized guru
pissed off by a grey skyscraper.
Moloch the incomprehensible prison!
Moloch the crossbone soulless jailhouse
and Congress of sorrows!
'Who's riding my ass? . . .
You come in a queer package, but you got guts.'
says the beast scratching its nose.

Moloch stands up, with its arms and ankles
decorated with bracelets set with gleaming jewels . . .
No, it's all bullshit, none of that, wait:
the giant, approximately 600 feet tall,
naked like chatterbox Ginsberg's ghost
is shaking off ground, mud and small hills
from its crocodile skin.
—Now you see it—
—Now you don't—
French and German soldiers slide down its shoulders
while the monster grabs some bayonets,

WAR

and old sharpened bones to pick its teeth.
The trenches, lying so still for months,
—the veins and the arteries of Moloch—
suddenly take off vertically
dripping down slowly like red honey,
quickly draining, weakening the beast
who rubs its still sleepy eyes.

Moloch salutes the horizon, over there
—it seems the world's oldest and biggest general—
where appear the ghosts of the future,
(white and skinny)
and those fresh with a pierced helmet,
(black, fat, with their souls still attached, like tails)
squashes some mosquitos
and lies down again, forming again the battlefield
for all those armed ant colonies,
dressed in bright red and blue uniforms,
belly up, now, with their little crazy paws
trying to catch a flag or a machine gun,
—maybe just one more day—
before everyone else.

SPECTRAL PERFUME
by Marge Simon

Her cloak thrown carelessly on the chair,
a field of rolling velvet hills where
up and down spiders swarm,
drawn to a decanter tinged
with garnet—Muguet from Paris,

created at the first of World War I,
and none to follow for a year—
the survivors might as well have
bought the scent of perfumed blood.

Certain songs of times gone by
of young men dying in the trenches,
with only crumpled memories of home,
letters scented with Muguet,
signatures in carmine kisses.

The air is thick with shadowed secrets—
like the single rose she puts beside
her precious, priceless perfume,
darkly sacred as her memories.

She never charged conscripted men,
forgets she died in 1924.

HUSH
by Alessandro Manzetti and Marge Simon

Hush.
Let me hear the rock and roll,
of the machine guns down there.
Sssssso sexy, man!
The slant-eyed princesses,
with necklaces of bullets around their thin necks,
singing love songs, looking so fine
in their green vietcong helmets.

I can see their lips moving . . .
*those whites so pearly,
the soft, red doors of Saigon
the petticoats of the jungle . . .*
You know what I'm talking about, right?
Every war has its fantasies,
dark eyed Sirens with verdant wings,
you hear them whispering promises,
smell their decadent perfume
above the stentch of death . . .

Hush. *Listen . . .*
Wow, this is a bazooka's blues . . .
but now, the music's changed—
that's all I need after all this rain,
that naked man on the crucifix,
is drowning in my boots
with his silver skeleton.
Come on, don't stop please,
we're only a few, out of ammo,
unsung heroes waiting to be saved

from another wet tomorrow,
with no more cigarettes,
not enough blood to walk.
Can you hear me girls?

Hey, don't look at me like that, brother,
haven't you seen a man in love?
Maybe you're surprised by that platoon
of Cinderellas waltzing out of the paddy field.
You'll see them soon.
How many days have you been here?

Hush, *Believe me.*
You have no idea how lucky you are,
to be dead yesterday,
dressed in a dry uniform,
before falling in love with death like me . . .
yeah, weirder than grooming a unicorn.

Hush, *don't move.*
They're arriving, with their sharp voices,
grains of rice in their hair
and a blade for me,
which shines like your silver tooth;
the only star survived here
hanging in your mouth wide open.

WAR

When Cortes doesn't answer,
she tosses the entrail back into the swirling waters.

Maria de Estrada, bloodied as the men,
her helmet gone, jaw swollen from a missing tooth,
comes to stand beside her captain.
The wind rises to dry the blood in her hair.
Your seer—the Dona, she warns we are not done,
she says, but Cortes shakes his head,
confounded that this woman fought
as well as any of his men, and lives.

La Noche es negra, y tiene grandes rubíes
entre sus dientes.
The embankments of the city, splattered with blood
suck the spicy flavor of slaughtered Spanish
while the children, with their yellow painted faces,
phosphorescent as road signs,
stand on the banks and the knees of the Calzadas
to fish with their hemp nets,
strangers' severed arms and hands
still clutching gold jewelry,
chipped rosaries and escaped moths
whose magic dust swirls in the air
in a rhapsody of wings' squamas
already flown away.

Who killed Montezuma sings the thrasher,
but the children are too busy with their task,
dark eyes shining.

IRAQI SUNSET
by Alessandro Manzetti

There are thin towers here,
of ivory and smoke,
and golden and yellowish domes
on the edge of the horizon;
I see mosques, the breasts of death
camped out between the mines,
and a fat sun, there in the middle
covered with the ruined orange fabric
of the tattered, gasping day.

My gaze starts to race
across the empty rooftops,
like a cat with the tail on fire;
it wants to join, with a leap into the void,
those flocks of mosquitoes
and helicopters with their steel, green leather
and a star attached to the belly
—the only one you can see here—
which are buzzing in the sky
alive with clothes hanging out to dry
and old iridescent carpets
stained with blood.

I close my eyes, imagining to fly
above that city, which can't tell
the living from the dead,
imagining to breast-feeding
the nacre ghost of my baby
—not the only one you can see here—
swallowed by a bomb crater
on the navel of an old fruit market.

GEORGE TECUMSEH SHERMAN'S GHOSTS
by Marge Simon

Poetry Winner of Rhysling Award 2017

Florida, 1914

Most nights, you mention him,
the ghosts rise from the cypress
come back to wail and moan.
Haints all look the same,
can't tell the whites from the Brothers,
'cause the war took every one alike,
and some still stick around.

It's been nigh fifty years, Granpappy say,
back when it was the Civil war,
and that man with crazy eyes came through—
old General Sherman and his men,
took our food, our mules,
even our women along the way,
burning and blazing every field,
cotton or corn or sugar cane,
telling us we join up,
so's we'd be free, that's what they said.

Granpappy almost starved,
beings how the soldiers got the food
and only scraps for the Brothers that survived;
still more drowned at Ebeneezer Creek
trying so hard to keep up,
a-marching straight to hell,
all the while still being slaves,
no better than the Reb's to them.

But them haints, General Sherman,
they all look the same.

THE BLACK SENTRY
by Alessandro Manzetti and Marge Simon

Santiago de Chile
September 11, 1973

Machopo river becomes black,
same thing for the crown of mountains
that tightens Santiago's forehead
without make turning upside down
squares, buildings, the bones of the saints
packaged in the Catedral
—like candy of Paradise—
where Pablo Neruda's ghost is hiding
waiting the death of its master,
the poet with so few days of life left
in his white shirt pocket.

Someone speaks of all that black,
which is covering everything, says it
comes from the veins of Queen Aconcagua,
Titi's undead wife, a living valley,
and that she's dragging her tail to the city
with an AK47 machine gun on the shoulder,
and on her face, a black mask of death
hand carved with lizard's heads,
pierced by her snowy eyes,
so white, white like the belly of Antartica.

She's heading to the Palacio de la Moneda
—*listen to me, that's how it must be*—
where Allende is waiting for her
inside his red Marxist robe
without hanging medals
and something good to trade.

WAR

The Black Sentry will suck his life
through a narrow straw, in one sitting
to crown another little king, a general,
a slave in double-breasted suits
with more lives on its conscience
and a thousand-pages book of tortures
like it was a Bible, a way to heaven.

Black as in black market economy,
black as in uniforms of the military officers
who lived apart in country club fashion,
married their children to their own;
black as the heart of Pinochet.

To the Santiago stadium two lines
were marched, of men and women alike—
one of stunned faces, the other at ease,
the lucky ones knew they'd be freed.

Huge fans started up to hide the sound
of the rat-tat-tat's sharp and sure,
so many guns, so short the time.
But when they saw, the people knew,
and they sang *The Internationale.*

ALICE IN HELL
by Alessandro Manzetti

Khan Bani Saad, Iraq
July 17, 2015

Death is as cold as ice,
and offers a discount, sometimes
like today, when the Iraqi sun
opening wide its orange mouth,
shows its teeth of ancient ivory,
the shrapnel of the artifacts
 just exploded at Nimrud,
and says to all "Burn!"

The market is crowded with people,
who still have their head attached to their neck
thin, dark willow branches
with green and white beads necklaces
wrapped around
and a small winged rock hanging:
a miniature of an Assyrian spirit
with half-bull and half-lion body,
cherubs wings on its stone shoulders,
solid and aerodynamic
as those of an American fighter aircraft,
and the face of a young king who died
five thousand years ago.

The truck of the Death, full of ice blocks
blows the horn 3 times
attracting the people with their tongue out
and the sandy-colored flies
form circles in the air
as if they were living, vibrant halos

WAR

looking for new saints of the desert
with stigmata that bleed oil.

Two USA marines laugh, with hot beer bottles
in the side pockets of their camouflaged trousers,
they're trading their lighters
for a talisman, a rosary with fake emerald grains
which protects against bullets and shells
sold by an old bearded Babylonian,
a resurrected priest, a son of Nineveh,
sitting on a rocking chair
near his rusted van.

A man darkened by the sun
is caressing his two goats
with human eyes and corroded fur
stained with blood roses,
while a woman is stretching blue fabrics
with her fingers painted purple,
a slice of her face framed
by black dunes sewn tight to each other.

The horn blows 3 times, again
threatening to leave.
"Jalid!" "Jalid!"
Rabia, twelve years old,
twelve dreams hidden under her yellow corsage
runs towards the truck of the Death
dragging her little brother;
she never saw a block of ice in one piece,
she never saw the ocean, the sea
a tap with hot and cold water.
An old man with a blindfolded eye
decorated with a red Pollock stain,
sees her and the other children run,
raises his shepherd's stick, and shouts . . .
But it's too late.

ALESSANDRO MANZETTI AND MARGE SIMON

The bomb screams like an insane dervish,
who cries out the lines of an apocalypse
appeared in dreams, liquefied in his blood,
spitting its 3 tons of explosive.
The truck raises its back
like a large circus animal,
then shoots fire from the wooden flanks,
ice powder, iron splinters
before disintegrating
and staining the asleep summer sky,
up there, where big lungs
are accustomed to the tobacco of souls
to their sweet aroma, reminiscent of vanilla,
of a sudden decapitation.

Rabia finds herself on the ground
with burning hair, in a suit of dust
sorrounded by the acid smell
of today that dies too soon,
before sunset, before the lullaby of the crickets
before the luminescences of the curfew
before she can catch something good
during the fertile, fat silence of night.
She raises her back and looks around;
Where is everyone? she thinks
Five, Four, Three, Two, One...
The storm of sirens is delaying . . .
while her mother's head rolls slowly
like a ball, toward her naked feet.
Rabia grabs it, stands up and begins to run
towards a hole in the smoke,
moving south, where the cardboard shingles
of the roof of her house appear,
close to the long leaves of a palm tree
which flowers hand bombs instead of dates.
She will keep her mother's head safe,
she will never forget her face.

WAR

—Not this time —
A ghost with big hands, without head
is already too much in that house
I miss you, Daddy!

WHITE SIEGE
by Alessandro Manzetti and Marge Simon

"Stalingrad is no longer a city.
By day it is a huge cloud of blinding smoke.
And when the night comes, dogs dive into the Volga,
because the nights of Stalingrad terrorize them.»
(Diary of a Soviet soldier)

Stalingrad, December 12, 1942

A woman is wearing a black coat
and snow jewels on her cold breasts;
She has crumbled bones,
and two children to feed,
up there, on the seventh floor
of the building, ornated
with the 24-carat holes
of the machine guns,
slaughtered like the last
giant hog on Earth
—a mirage of flesh —
after so much hunger,
and long times of mud meatballs
and gas broth.

A German Panzer
is lying in the middle of the street,
looks like a mammoth
without teeth and fur,
that barely breathes,
inflating its veins and tracks.
It swallowed its Aryan driver
—cooked by molotov —
one week ago,

and is still digesting
his square jaws and iron medals.

An old man near a stack of boots
with a blanket on his head
and a bullet in his brain,
convinced he is dead,
is crawling on all fours,
—sniffing his nephew's red t-shirt—
listening to the grenade's jazz
and the barking of dogs—
their tails in flames that illuminate
the shadows of the street,
macabre, elusive traces
of what once was.

Mamochka stewed our dog,
but Yeva was very thin,
so his meat was spare.
Our baby brother,
born after the troops came,
he is too weak to eat, doesn't
cry, his diaper goes unused.
There are three of us to feed,
Mama has no choice.

Winter's wedding ring,
a red bruise around her neck.
In the mirror a full bellied man's refection
that moves like a mad monkey in his guts,
chasing him to the white building
on the paradox corner fragmented
by the blast of his blame, his wife's remains
still screaming in his stomach.

White souls, white uniforms
white weapons, white pain

WAR

(the shock of each dawn)
eating snow, while Beauty
is trapped in a block of ice
with mouth open, arms still up
(shouting 'please, just stop this!')
and frozen hairs sticking out
from the roots of dreams,
white like a painting just started.
While they're dying. 'Why?'
(asked a little girl in front of a big pot)
A whine, out there. Then a thousand.
It's the White Siege soundtrack.

Beyond the city,
Winter wears long hands,
miles of white on the horizon.
We've become stickmen in uniform,
sunken faced and hollow eyed;
hunger clawing at our guts
like a cat trapped in a bag.
We no longer feel the cold.

Kreuger falls, won't get up, won't talk.
He's been sick for days,
frostbite has claimed his feet,
already he smells like a dead thing.
As we stand around him,
Bucholdst begins tapping his bowl
against his bayonet.
I won't let us start on him
before his last breath.
Das Fuhrer would appove,
it is a matter of pride.

THE SOUTHERN LADY
by Marge Simon

With death, there should be dignity
but there is none here. Soldiers in dusty blues
trample on my precious roses, bleeding
their perfume into the soil. And those half dead
are brought to my parlor, soaking my fine
couches with their Yankee blood.

Cow and calf alike they shot for practice up in Charleston,
by the time they got to ours, they wanted bread and butter,
with pitchers of fresh milk to wash it down;
some seem surprised there's none.
They'd burned our fields, there was no feed,
did they think our livestock lived on love?

I dreamed I was a giant cat,
sitting on a wounded soldier's chest
watching him quietly while he slept,
then I leapt on his face and clawed out his eyes.

But he rose up, playing "*Aura Lee*" on his harmonica.
One by one, his companions joined in singing,
and we danced all around the room.
Beyond the window it was raining blood.

MISS SAIGON
by Alessandro Manzetti and Marge Simon

Saigon, Summer 1969

Lin Hoa is dancing for us
dressed in a leather miniskirt
showing her teenage breasts
by raising and lowering
her t-shirt that says
'Black Clap' in golden letters.
She's playing with us, she smiles
and grabs my beer to have a little sip;
a healthy 14-year-old girl like her,
with those perfect white teeth,
can't host the black eggs of syphilis.
It's still too early for her,
even in this overturned paradise,
in this city where dust
doesn't have time to settle down
before disappearing
dragged away together with the corpses.

'300 piastres',
she whispers into my ears,
and then into those of my drunken comrades,
their hands shaking in attempts
to capture non-existant black butterflies
— it's not time to pull the trigger, dude!—
circling the red light bulbs
up there, hanging above
this luminescent roof of Saigon,
so far from the jungle.

darkened by the open mouth
of a hungry ground.
But death can wait, over there
with its shining helmet of tomorrow
which we mistake for a new moon.

Upstairs in a certain yellow room
with a pink radio tuned to Radio Hanoi,
I discover that Lin Hoa
has a special moon of her own
tattooed around her navel.
She giggles when I touch it,
pushes my face down to her crotch.
begging me to enter her special place,
so tight, so fresh and new,
she moans and says I'm the best
she's ever known as my dick meets
the razor blades within her sweet young cunt.
Through a mist or red hot pain, I'm aware
before she disappears, she upps the volume,
Hendrix blasting Purple Haze
to drown out my screams.

I know I won't be pulling any trigger,
should have been chasing
those black butterflies
instead of Saigon tail.

TEN TO ONE
by Alessandro Manzetti

March 24 1944

I'm the grass snake of the past,
look at my black, gold and silver skin;
You've never seen me before?
I'm what sparkles down here
on the horizon, at a distance
where old things lie
where memories and carcasses
seek their own grave
or new life, some fuel to run again
into foreign hearts,
into the yet unborn chests
of the future's ghosts.

I'm what crawls next to your feet,
look around, what do you see?
Rome, your city, cleaned by blood,
your new shoes, capable of going to Mars,
white bread in the shop windows,
mouths with all their teeth still whole
and two fake Roman legionnaires
with their plastic swords.
You can't see anything but all this, right?
If you could read my mind . . .
and see what's in the stomach of this city,
below, between the fangs of this chimera.

But maybe there is a way, listen to me.
Follow me, you can do it.
You'll be a grass snake like me, for an hour
and get into this manhole

WAR

leading into the bowels of Via Ardeatina.
We'll crawl together,
you'll quickly learn how to use your new tail
and discover the secret of the ventral scales
before arriving at the quarries,
which still smell
of Kappler's and Priebke's adrenaline
of nazi gunpowder and dynamite.
Follow me, you can do it.

Now stop here, we have to turn right:
but be careful, the corpses are packed like ingots
and the tunnel is very narrow.
You could be trapped in there
like all those who can't forget,
with rusted hooks under their skin,
like all those buried here
with worms like lovers
and the soul of a companion to drink.
Ten to one, do you remember now?
You can do it.

---

*Ten Italians for every German killed in a partisan attack on SS officers as they marched through Rome; such was General Malzer's decree. It was approved by Hitler, who added that the reprisal must be within twenty-four hours. In their rush to comply, SS soldiers rounded up both prisoners and innocent Italian civilians. The ending number was greater than called for. All of them were executed and buried in a cave. The event is known as the Ardeatine Massacre, and stands symbolic of heinous injustices committed on Italian civilians by German soldiers until Hitler's surrender in May, 1945.

THE GHOSTS OF CULLODEN: 1746
by Marge Simon

Can you hear them, can you see them
Marching proudly across the moor,
Hear the wind blow thru the drifting snow,
Tell me can you see them, the ghosts of Culloden.

                      lines from "The Ghosts of Culloden" by Isla Grant

A savage lot, you say,
wearing kilts their women wove,
the dyes set by their lasses' piss.
Look close to see the weave,
their tartans fine as any noble's vest.

Can you see them, rising up again
with their claymores dipped in red,
but when the smoke of battle clears,
they fade into the mist.

And all to unify the clans,
to return the Stuart line
to England's throne.
Such a waste of lives—
their Bonnie Prince Charles
was a fucking arse.

Climb to the Highlands
to find the standing stones,
make passage back in time,
then feel the thunderous entry
of their passing souls—
and you can worship down.

WAR

There is a bloodied page
in this history tome I hold.
I am a daughter
among daughters of many.
We'd have fought too,
if such were allowed.

We carry the weight
of suppressed rain,
the loss of lands,
the seasons of death
etched in the planes
of our faces.

This page you may scribe on,
so many lies on,
but no pen can change
nor words rearrange
what happened at Culloden.

THE MAN WHO WOULD BE KING
by Alessandro Manzetti

Nuremberg, October 15, 1946

King Hermann looks at his past
from the window of the cell
lit by an imaginary crystal chandelier,
the transparent constellation
of his new home chock-full
of ticks that suck only white blood,
the thoughts of the prisoners
rotate in their heads
like submarine propellers
swirling the water of the main lake:
the cerebral fluid.

King Hermann sees out there
his enchanted garden,
surrounded by barbed wire,
and the shadow of his favorite tiger
with blue and gold stripes,
which jumps between iron flowers,
catching a wingless bird
with human head;
—*Hey! You're wrong!*—
shouts the little man
miniaturized into a Eurasian collared dove
covered with red feathers,
and a Star of David tied around his neck.

Above an altar, between two ash trees
that sweat black manna, like sun-baked rubber,
King Hermann admires his shiny crown,
and, beside it, his Renaissance dagger,

WAR

encrusted with diamonds, emeralds
and eyes of slaves, of Jewish pigs,
who are still staring at their young death:
a twenty year old girl approaching them
indefinitely, with her scent of mango and instinct,
an armed virgin dressed like Wagner's Brunhilde,
with wings on the helmet and a long spear
able to pierce and plague, every time,
the livers of inferior races.

In that sky so yellow,
yellow as the illusions hard to break,
King Hermann can see in the distance
his old World War I biplane flying,
and singing with its machine guns
while the fat Mercedes engine
tunes the sounds of arrogance, and immortality.
—Here it is, coming back to me—
A lion cub bites his boots,
and a golden cigarette case falls on the floor
sounding like the last round bell.

Past can't swallow other days,
the enchanted garden disappears, out there,
and now King Hermann sees himself
reflected on the window glass
wearing too wide white funeral gloves,
a noose around his flushed neck
and a black medal pinned on the chest.
—It's not me—
He crunches a cyanide candy between his teeth,
the medicine of the Kings;

Wagner's music resumes playing
leading him towards the Great Pit
where the choir of the dead
is waiting for him.

THE CEMETERY WAR: BOOT HILL
by Marge Simon

At moonrise
above the dirt saloon
specters share stories,
the faded music of Babylon
whistled to the wind
through rotting teeth.

Painted lady phantoms
do the bump and grind,
a seductive dance
with filmy scarves
of dermal skin,
then ectoderm,
down to the bone.

Death visits to celebrate
with a breath of whiskey,
a reminder of conflicts
over women, gold, land,
moths and moonbeams.

The action starts at midnight,
wails, moans, shrieks, groans,
a clash of souls beyond redemption,
damned to war in purgatory,
the stench of rotten tangerines.

It's over just before
the honking horns
of alabaster chariots
disturb the sunrise.

POP 9/11
by Alessandro Manzetti

Like hundred-pound piranhas,
we bite pieces of day
with an eternally empty stomach.
We are brigades, and we are already extinct
before the light turns red.
Our queen Rush, with her long blue fins
and the yellow smile of an imaginary sun
flashing, newborn and just dead,
she laid her soft eggs under the skyscrapers
which continue to grow, up to pierce
the fucking fake sky, the aquarium lid.
Each of us has a golden phone
to speak at any time
with a psychoanalyst or a new god
but nobody hears the fat cries,
far and near, of the ambulances,
of the bombing across the pond
which whizzes through the alleys of TV news
aboard the psychedelic Janis Joplin's porsche.

We are millions in this Coke Sea,
with the engine of boredom turned on
and commercial jingles in the ears.
As piranhas we bite thousands of images
without really seeing them:
A homeless man in his shorts, in the middle of the street
with his beard scorched by dementia,
is waving the Confederate flag
while Manhattan repeatedly dodges it
passing him next to seventy miles an hour.
At the same time

someone has a heart attack on Wall Street,
deflates his elegant double-breasted jacket
and from the sewn by hand pocket protrude
the brown head of a Cuban cigar
and a bags of cocaine.
Andy Warhol's ghost
with a blue wig and tortoise sunglasses,
who understood the trick a long time ago,
continue to record the images
of the Empire State Building,
the greatest still life of all time,
without losing a grain, a leap
or a perfect pirouette
of Now which is dancing for everyone.

As piranhas we attack in groups,
we just need to smell the fresh meat;
Jezebel, the Phoenician princess
the high-priced whore with her red skirt
and a leash studded with amethysts
leaves her apartment carrying
a network full of fish, caudal fins, dollars,
and winks at the pimp on the corner
who's counting the money
with a Lucky Strike in his mouth,
humming his rap,
just turning his head towards the rumble.
The plane, like a huge razor
cut the sky, chopping off the cable of the morning
making it fall on us, like thick rain
tons of Campbell tomato sauce
and the red fliers of what so far
had passed before our eyes

to die later, after the first corner
in the subway station

WAR

for an overdose of indifference
in front of a wall painted by Keith Haring
where he shows us all as men and women.

DRUG WARS: FOUR POEMS
by Marge Simon

Grim Guests

Taos, 1968
a certain country house
overlooks the sun scorched desert.
It is wonderfully cool inside,
with beautiful floors of sienna tiles
and expensive minimalist furnishings.

To this house comes a black sedan
covered in thick yellow dust from
across the southern border.
Five men emerge bearing suitcases,
four of them are the color of the tiles.
They wear sunglasses,
guns holstered inside suits.
The pale one with yellow hair
speaks English and sits
at the head of the table.

The bong is lit,
the flavor of the day
is Acapulco Gold,
but the bargain
is for snow.

A deal goes down,
in a special language familiar
to all gathered.
No names mentioned,
no questions asked.
The child of the hosts

WAR

is not permitted in the room,
but he can smell and hear
what is going on.

Years later, as a top agent
for a pharmaceutical company,
he makes drug deals
less intense, highly profitable;
often deadly, totally legal.

Carrots and Sticks

A boy named Santos knows
how to plant carrots and sticks
to fool the men in green uniforms.

The real plunder is deep in a nature preserve
where fumigation cannot touch its precious bounty
and no government nor Medellin cartel
will choke his livelihood.

Once there were promises
of help for farmers if they
raised legal crops in place of coca.
But when the farmers did as asked,
and planted cane and corn
no help ever came

Mornings Santos plucks a leaf,
chews and dreams of fortune.
He is a grown man now.
He is no fool.

Heavy Weather

Maria lives in Nuevo Laredo.
She awakes early to get her son
dressed and off to preschool.
She checks her social media feed
for news of the latest murder.

Always, there is the weather to think of.
It doesn't rain water there, it rains lead,
viper kisses any time of day or night,
far from the rainforest,
yet a jungle all the same.

It is part of Maria's life,
part of her little boy's life;
he will accept it as she has,
this life in the civilized wild,
it is the way things are.

Prison

It wasn't a big deal,
maybe just some lids—
rent money, whatever,
you knew people,
they knew people.

You didn't expect to be caught
selling those baggies, but you were.
There was more afterwards,
like your mom crying and your dad
not meeting your eyes, not talking.

You didn't expect to be stripped
and sprayed and shoved into a cell

WAR

with a guy built like the Terminator
and what he did to you later,

he and his friends.
You never were into sports,
but you learned how it felt
to entertain the team,
dancing at half time
naked in the stark lights,
one fucked up mascot
for two years.

When they let you out,
pointed you to the gate,
pride in shreds, broken—
none of it made sense.
It was only weed, man,
only fucking weed.

BLACK RAY
by Alessandro Manzetti and Marge Simon

Prinzenregentplatz 27, Monaco
April 30, 1945

Lee takes off her dirty boots
filled with Dachau's mud
and gets in the Hitler's bathtub
blending her polarized skin,
the golden powder of a surrealist muse
and a necklace of sea sponges,
with that still virgin water,
which seems to be waiting for an angel
after serving so long a cold demon
without gills, blood and sperm
enduring the awful perfume,
—like snake oil—
of its former owner.

Lee's breast, turned into a living reef,
half submerged in that reddish foam,
is surrounded by eddies of memories
— and by the tongues of the dead
she saw in the concentration camp —
headed to her mind, so quickly.
Hundreds of photo shoots,
human fences, charred voices
and a patchwork of forgotten faces
floating in the river, near there
like a flexible armor encrusted with eyes.

Then a familiar face appear,
it's him, Man Ray, the rider of the absurd
—he looks good wearing that tinfoil hat —

He shows her a wedding dress,
white, sewn with fishing nets,
and then a army uniform, black,
with golden teeth instead of buttons.
"*You choose, princess*", he whispers
before vanishing like bath salts,
blue, melting around her thighs,
in that bathtub of the monster,
the same as any other.

*She remembers the wounds
after a bath with him and leaving
him dripping wet on his own.
She dreams of painting him
black on black.*

She stands to towel dry,
feeling dirty all over again,
marked with dark sludge,
like those faces at Dachau
that won't wash away.

CHOCOLATES FOR TWINS
by Marge Simon

Auschwitz, 1943

Crows circle the skies above the rails,
searching for splattered remains
of those who ask too many questions,
or bits of a small child's chocolates.

From crowded boxcars pour
the newest visitors to Camp Auschwitz.
Josef Mengele stands on the platform.
His hat is cocked, his boots shine like mirrors.

He surveys his prey, conducts the order of their fate.
With a bronze tipped cane he waves most to the right
to be cleansed by cyanide showers,
directs the fittest to the left, for various tasks.

Uncle was the first to welcome us,
with bright eyes and shining smiles
for me and my twin sister Yael,
he made us feel so special,
giving us each a chocolate treat,
he whisked us off in his private car.

He said our parents would visit soon—
though they were shown to the left,
we had no clue what that meant.
So Yael and I settled in,
glad to be safe in a place
for Hebrew pairs like us.
Very soon our world became a window
into Uncle Mengele's orchestrated Hell,

yet in our innocence, we tried to please.
Amir and Miriam were injected with smallpox;
the nurses made us drink their blood while
Uncle Mengele supervised, a glitter in his eyes.

With special chocolates for twins!

To Yankel and Yoel,
he injected certain chemicals
to change the color of their eyes
from brown to blue; he didn't stop
until they both went blind.

More chocolates as rewards.

Ezra and Emmanel
were sewn together,
unnatural Siamese twins,
but their hands got infected
and they were put to death
in a certain room he used
for duteous dissection.

Chocolates to celebrate.

He pricked Shaindel's eardrums
until she could barely hear
snapped her sister Moira's legs,
and crushed her feet
to study if they cared
about each other's fate
before they died.

We didn't want the chocolates.

Johan's story was as sad,
Uncle operated on his brother's spine,

WAR

so his legs were paralyzed,
and removed his sex parts—
probably some other things as well.
Death came the fourth time.
He didn't see his brother after that.

He wouldn't eat the chocolates.

Uncle switched the heads
of Joprie and Shoshanna,
we saw them on the cart.

No chocolates for them.

Such tests went on with
Uncle Mengele's special treats
in between the operations
for those of us still living,
and if we knew what befell
the ones who never returned
we dared not speak of it.

So when the day came,
to save gas, and still alive,
we were thrown into the ovens,
it didn't matter.

We knew enough,
we'd had enough
of Uncle Mengele's chocolates.

HOLY DIVER
by Alessandro Manzetti

Beit Hanoun, April 28, 2008

The Israeli cannon coughs,
it has too much sand in its throat.
It missed the target, shooting too high,
between the yellow sky and the boxes
of the Beit Hanoun refugee camp.
Rats escape in all directions,
like stars with tails and too many paws,
suddenly divided into parts,
making their muscles explode.
Cockroaches open their primitive wings
and fly away from the ruins of the house;
they look like like black raindrops,
falling backwards,
reflecting the flames on their shiny shells
while they cross the Gaza Strip
which cannot be seen from above,
which does not exist.

The Abu Matek family, five heads in all,
fills the hallway, the two small rooms
with their Palestinian blood, light red,
painting the cardboard ceilings
with soft brain's arabesques
and spatter of pink, yellow, and silver dreams
without borders and homeland.
Fatima, the mother of the four children,
a Virgin Mary with dark and empty breasts
and a smile without teeth,
who sucks dates and swallows their bones,
is the only survivor of the grenade.
Musaab, one year old, Salah, four years old,

WAR

Hana five years, Rudeina six years old;
her sons and daughters, angels with curly hair,
tattooed by the sun and a curse
cut to pieces, scattered everywhere
like pomegranate seeds
freed from their peel.

The cardboard walls of the house
tilt down towards the center
making the blood pour down the hallway
as a dense red river,
fed by such young sources and tributaries
where fins of human organs
draw macabre circles and ovals
with invisible fingers,
intertwining as pieces of ancient chains
wanting to reunite again.

Fatima, without legs,
blown away along with the cockroaches
outside the kitchen mosquito net,
dives into that purple, gurgling funnel,
that hallway turned into a new uterus
for her already born children,
to give birth to them again, all together
the same day, in a new land
without stripes and borders,
militiamen and soldiers,
and too many sacred bricks.

Fatima holds her breath,
swimming in that water dense as ink,
then, tired, she opens her mouth,
making the red river find her lungs,
waiting for the eight hands of the children
to grab her, pushing her body to the bottom
which does not exist.

THE CASTRATO'S PARADE
by Marge Simon

The eunuchs paraded for rights, today.
Legions of dour men
marching in clipped unison
on a cold November afternoon
with neither bands nor majorettes,

nor clowns in little wagons,
only their leader astride a white mule.
You turn to me, a question in your eyes,
but I put a finger on your lips.

Silently, we watch them
proceed down Broadway
until they diminish from view.
Onlookers unify in a mighty sigh
and return to go about their business.

Later we discuss this in bed,
my arms embracing your shoulders,
your legs twined in mine.

"Was it to make a statement,
to gain recognition, acceptance?"
"I suppose it was," I reply.
"We started all this, didn't we, Flora,
eons ago? Why do you frown?"

"I guess they expect equal rights, too."
"It won't happen in our lifetime, love!" I say,
pulling your hands to encircle my breasts.

We kiss with tenderness as only women do.

I lie awake afraid to fall asleep. I know those
austere faces will invade my dreams.

YBYI 21
APOCALYPSE TOMORROW
by Alessandro Manzetti

ESCAPE

The motor of the dinghy is frying,
it smells of gasoline and death, like everything else.
I look at the coast that goes away,
behind us, behind the survivors.
Asunción cradles her headless daughter,
she sings something moving her scorched lips.
Mauricio draws a mermaid of blood on his skin
with the shining blade of his machete.
Catalina ties her ripped out guts
and distractedly makes a nice bow of flesh.
The island's outlines materializes, down on the right
like a ghost battleship with a weird living tail;
it's followed by a long line of small boats
stuffed with dead flesh and the juice of fear.
They're seeking salvation, like us,
floating on red water, contaminated by human entrails—
the new skin of the sea, the tattoo of the Apocalypse.

Hector, the old man, stands up,
gets out of his ragged clothes
and beats his fists on his chest,
cursing the new sky that threatens again
to piss fire and hydrochloric acid.
If it starts raining, we're screwed, melted to the bone.
But Hector seems to be able to talk with that damned sky,
he faces it hard-nosed, challenging it.
With his unnaturally unscrewed jaws, he starts to cry,
blowing his words hard between the broken molars,
those teeth which have not chewed meat for two years.

ALESSANDRO MANZETTI AND MARGE SIMON

Our captain slows down the dinghy,
and presses his blue eyes into the binoculars.
He tells us about the island, about what he can see
and what he wants to make us imagine,
whispers wonders to keep us alive.
My mind returns to the mainland, sinking feet
in the blood of the slaughterhouse of the harbor,
where people kill each other to get
the latest safe passages to the island,
where the mutated rats, big as sows,
are making a mess of fresh meat.
They're the new gods of this world,
with their tails and an infinite stomach,
forged by stars and sewers.
You can see a new kind of deluge over there,
emerging from the manholes like a tide,
the red foam of the old owners of the world—
HUMANS.

The boiling rain will soon clean all this shit,
leaving room for new highways, covered
with white, polished bones.
The weird rainbow that overlooks the harbor
with its acid psychedelic yellow and green,
a remnant of Pompeii, Chernobyl,
Hiroshima, everything put together.
You only need to escape,
getting your passage to the island
—called the Pacific Trash Vortex—
and whoever is up in the front row ahead of you
is your number one enemy.
Ybyi 21 Year 0.6, this is our calendar,
for those lucky enough to have counted so long
after the impact of the meteor.

On our dinghy we feel a desperation
which is revealing as a seasickness of the soul.

WAR

Silvanio tells the story of Calypso,
the phantom of the Apocalypse.
Everyone is listening to him,
even the headless daughter of Asunción
with her neck's purple root that continues to spit blood.
Someone has woken the ghost, Calypso,
says the fat whoremonger,
rubbing his beard, showing his ruby ring on his little finger,
well before the meteor and kaboom of the Kaesŏng,
the queen of the rats and of the end of everything.

From the leather belt of our weird captain
hangs a rosary composed of severed human fingers,
that's how he was paid to take you to the Island.
Since the meteor fucked planet Earth,
twenty grams of non-infected proteins
are worth more than a gold bar.
Twenty fingers, twenty passengers,
twenty survivors, twenty grams of protein.

BOMBING

On the muzzle of the bomber is painted
a shark's smile that seems to chew the clouds.
The Colonel, the pilot, pushes the engines past maximum,
the shadow of his steel bird rustled on the wheat fields,
gutted by the thousand craters
of the tails of meteor Ybyi 21.
Then a few seconds later the aluminum palisades
of the village materializes.
The watchtowers of the central bunker,
form an imaginary V,
as well as the buildings of warehouses and common rooms.
It's where the motherfuckers took refuge—
they're the kibbutz rats, the Taliban of conception
who don't comply with the 'zero' legislation

which prevents new births, after the Fist Impact.
There is not enough food for all.
The anti-aircraft of the Taliban begins
to spit fire on the bomber,
but the steel shark of the Colonel is too fast for them
and is already flying over the village,
when the hot necklaces of the bullets try to reach
a neck, the target, the flying enemy.

The Colonel leaves the automatic pilot in charge,
he sees the yellow horizon in front of him,
and the goal behind his ass,
between the gas tanks of the bomber
Shit! But there is still time.
He descends the ladder, jumps down and plants his feet
on the belly of his flying beast.
The bomb B71,
with *Fuck Your Bloodsucker Babies* painted over it
already armed and positioned on the floating cart,
and suspended above the hatch is so beautiful—
sexy, like a woman who hides in her belly so many secrets,
a Marylin Monroe, a 20th century Aphrodite,
pregnant with her own beauty, and nothing else.
The Colonel caresses the bomb, smiles, and thinks how B71
is like the explosive medicine of a stern Lord of Justice,
something good to treat the arrogance
of the reproducing the human species
on a planet so on the ropes.

Riding the B71, tied by safety belts,
the Colonel unhooks and jumps into the void,
increasingly accelerating toward the ground,
—*Hey, maybe it's another meteor ready to hit the planet*—
toward those bastards entrenched in the village,
with their disgustingly pregnant women,
nothing but sows with fallopian tubes wide open to fate,
and the armored silos of poppers which swarm and smell

WAR

of synthetic goat milk, derived from an heretic
molecular backbone, composed of 70% oil and rosamio.
We've many apocalyptic kinds of arsenic and venom here.
Even some of them seems to bring life, for a while.
The damn breeding, down there one thousand feet.
Living weeds, thinks the Colonel,
it would take a fucking gigantic chainsaw
to cut the grass of the planet properly.
We need B71 now to burst the Boil down there.
Six hundred feet above the ground
he feels an erection inflate the pants of his camouflage suit
and open-mouthed, he tastes the salty air for the last time.
The sea over there and the synthetic giant island
emerging from the North like a WW2 Japanese battleship,
The Pacific Trash Vortex,
is nothing but floating waste accumulated for years,
which has developed a primitive collective consciousness
and thousands of eyes, ears and mouths.
It can trace your smell,
up to hundreds of miles from the coast.
That New Continent, a next-gen predator,
pushes the engines to take up space
with propellers made of guts,
sun-baked and hard as leather.
The monster island grows every day
drinking the juice-mash of itself.
That new floating continent without floor and roots
will soon cover the Old Word as a tick blanket,
thousands of miles long.

Two hundred feet above the ground,
the Colonel tightens a Cuban cigar between his teeth,
he's bent by centrifugal force, but he doesn't give up
until near to the impact he achieves an orgasm,
a golden ray which passes through him, part-to-part,
making him feel like a new kind of Prometheus,
just before crashing and baptizing a beautiful chasm.

ALESSANDRO MANZETTI AND MARGE SIMON

When the cries cease and the babies' crumbs
feed new fruit trees and crops of blue strawberries,
surely they will give his name to that hole.
Once, people cared to classify the stars.
But that was long ago.

WAR

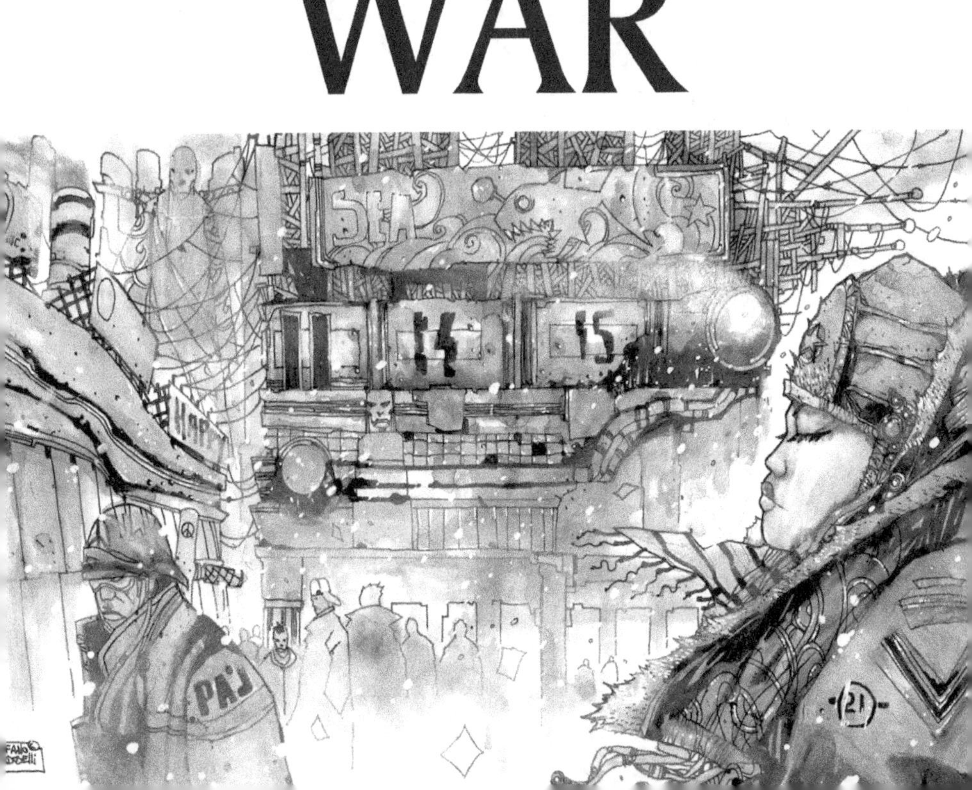

About the Authors

Marge Simon lives in Ocala, FL. She edits a column for the HWA Newsletter, "Blood & Spades: Poets of the Dark Side," and serves on Board of Trustees. She is the second woman to be acknowledged by the SF &F Association with a Grand Master Award. She has won the Bram Stoker Award, the Rhysling Award, Elgin, Dwarf Stars and Strange Horizons Readers' Award. Marge's poems and stories have appeared in Silver Blade, Bete Noire, Urban Fantasist, Daily Science Fiction, *You, Human, Chiral Mad 2,3,4* and *The Beauty Of Death Vol. 1* and *2*—to name a few. She attends the ICFA annually as a guest poet/writer and is on the board of the Speculative Literary Foundation.
www.margesimon.com

Alessandro Manzetti live in Trieste (Italy). He is the author of more than twenty books in English and Italian, including works of fiction, poetry, and nonfiction. His poems and stories have appeared in *Dark Moon Digest, The Horror Zine, Disturbed Digest, Illumen, Devolution Z, Recompose, Polu Texni, Bones III, Rhysling Anthology (2015, 2016, 2017, 2018), Hwa Poetry Showcase Vol. 3* and *4, The Beauty Of Death Vol. 1* and *2, Best Hardcore Horror Of The Year Vol. 2*—to name a few. His poetry collection *Eden Underground* won the Bram Stoker Award 2015, and his poetry collections *Venus Intervention* (with Corrine De Winter), *Sacrificial Nights* (with Bruce Boston) and *No Mercy* were nominated for the Bram Stoker Award.
www.battiago.com

The end?

Not quite . . .

Dive into more Tales from the Darkest Depths:

Novels:
Beyond Night by Eric S. Brown and Steven L. Shrewsbury
The Third Twin: A Dark Psychological Thriller by Darren Speegle
Aletheia: A Supernatural Thriller by J.S. Breukelaar
Beatrice Beecham's Cryptic Crypt: A Supernatural Adventure/Mystery Novel by Dave Jeffery
Where the Dead Go to Die by Mark Allan Gunnells and Aaron Dries
Sarah Killian: Serial Killer (For Hire!) by Mark Sheldon
The Final Cut by Jasper Bark
Blackwater Val by William Gorman
Pretty Little Dead Girls: A Novel of Murder and Whimsy by Mercedes M. Yardley
Nameless: The Darkness Comes by Mercedes M. Yardley

Novellas:
House of Sighs by Aaron Dries
Quiet Places: A Novella of Cosmic Folk Horror by Jasper Bark
The Final Reconciliation by Todd Keisling
Run to Ground by Jasper Bark
Devourer of Souls by Kevin Lucia
Apocalyptic Montessa and Nuclear Lulu: A Tale of Atomic Love by Mercedes M. Yardley
Wind Chill by Patrick Rutigliano
Little Dead Red by Mercedes M. Yardley
Sleeper(s) by Paul Kane
Stuck On You by Jasper Bark

Anthologies:

C.H.U.D. Lives!
Tales from The Lake Vol.4: The Horror Anthology, edited by Ben Eads
Behold! Oddities, Curiosities and Undefinable Wonders, edited by Doug Murano
Twice Upon an Apocalypse: Lovecraftian Fairy Tales, edited by Rachel Kenley and Scott T. Goudsward
Tales from The Lake Vol.3, edited by Monique Snyman
Gutted: Beautiful Horror Stories, edited by Doug Murano and D. Alexander Ward
Tales from The Lake Vol.2, edited by Joe Mynhardt, Emma Audsley, and RJ Cavender
Children of the Grave
The Outsiders
Tales from The Lake Vol.1, edited by Joe Mynhardt
Fear the Reaper, edited by Joe Mynhardt
For the Night is Dark, edited by Ross Warren

Short story collections:

Frozen Shadows and Other Chilling Stories by Gene O'Neill
Ugly Little Things: Collected Horrors by Todd Keisling
Whispered Echoes by Paul F. Olson
Embers: A Collection of Dark Fiction by Kenneth W. Cain
Visions of the Mutant Rain Forest, by Bruce Boston and Robert Frazier
Tribulations by Richard Thomas
Eidolon Avenue: The First Feast by Jonathan Winn
Flowers in a Dumpster by Mark Allan Gunnells
The Dark at the End of the Tunnel by Taylor Grant
Through a Mirror, Darkly by Kevin Lucia
Things Slip Through by Kevin Lucia
Where You Live by Gary McMahon
Tricks, Mischief and Mayhem by Daniel I. Russell
Samurai and Other Stories by William Meikle
Stuck On You and Other Prime Cuts by Jasper Bark

Poetry collections:

Brief Encounters with My Third Eye by Bruce Boston

No Mercy: Dark Poems by Alessandro Manzetti
Eden Underground: Poetry of Darkness by Alessandro Manzetti

If you've ever thought of becoming an author, we'd also like to recommend these non-fiction titles:

Where Nightmares Come From: The Art of Storytelling in the Horror Genre, edited by Joe Mynhardt and Eugene Johnson
Horror 101: The Way Forward, edited by Joe Mynhardt and Emma Audsley
Horror 201: The Silver Scream Vol.1 and *Vol.2*, edited by Joe Mynhardt and Emma Audsley
Modern Mythmakers: 35 interviews with Horror and Science Fiction Writers and Filmmakers by Michael McCarty
Writers On Writing: An Author's Guide Volumes 1,2,3, and 4, edited by Joe Mynhardt. Now also available in a Kindle and paperback omnibus.

Or check out other Crystal Lake Publishing books for more Tales from the Darkest Depths.

Hi, readers. It makes our day to know you reached the end of our book. Thank you so much. This is why we do what we do every single day.

Whether you found the book good or great, we'd love to hear what you thought. Please take a moment to leave a review on Amazon, Goodreads, or anywhere else readers visit. Reviews go a long way to helping a book sell, and will help us to continue publishing quality books. You can also share a photo of yourself holding this book with the hashtag #IGotMyCLPBook!

Thank you again for taking the time to journey with Crystal Lake Publishing.

We are also on . . .

Website:
www.crystallakepub.com

Be sure to sign up for our newsletter and receive two free eBooks: http://eepurl.com/xfuKP

Books:
http://www.crystallakepub.com/book-table/

Twitter:
https://twitter.com/crystallakepub

Facebook:
https://www.facebook.com/Crystallakepublishing/
https://www.facebook.com/Talesfromthelake/
https://www.facebook.com/WritersOnWritingSeries/

Pinterest:
https://za.pinterest.com/crystallakepub/

Instagram:
https://www.instagram.com/crystal_lake_publishing/

Patreon:
https://www.patreon.com/CLP

YouTube:
https://www.youtube.com/c/CrystalLakePublishing

We'd love to hear from you.

Or check out other Crystal Lake Publishing books for your Dark Fiction, Horror, Suspense, and Thriller needs.

With unmatched success since 2012, Crystal Lake Publishing has quickly become one of the world's leading indie publishers of Mystery, Thriller, and Suspense books with a Dark Fiction edge.

Crystal Lake Publishing puts integrity, honor and respect at the forefront of our operations.

We strive for each book and outreach program that's launched to not only entertain and touch or comment on issues that affect our readers, but also to strengthen and support the Dark Fiction field and its authors.

Not only do we publish authors who are legends in the field and as hardworking as us, but we look for men and women who care about their readers and fellow human beings. We only publish the very best Dark Fiction, and look forward to launching many new careers.

We strive to know each and every one of our readers, while building personal relationships with our authors, reviewers, bloggers, pod-casters, bookstores and libraries.

Crystal Lake Publishing is and will always be a beacon of what passion and dedication, combined with overwhelming teamwork and respect, can accomplish: Unique fiction you can't find anywhere else.

We do not just publish books, we present you worlds within your world, doors within your mind, from talented authors who sacrifice so much for a moment of your time.

This is what we believe in. What we stand for. This will be our legacy.

Welcome to Crystal Lake Publishing—Tales from the Darkest Depths

www.ingramcontent.com/pod-product-compliance
Lightning Source LLC
Chambersburg PA
CBHW071217070526
44584CB00019B/3059